In My
Egotistical
Opinion

A Lifetime of Wisdom Is Available Here

HARLEN KOEN

WESTBOW
PRESS®
A DIVISION OF THOMAS NELSON
& ZONDERVAN

WestBow Press books may be ordered through booksellers or by contacting:

WestBow Press
A Division of Thomas Nelson & Zondervan
1663 Liberty Drive
Bloomington, IN 47403
www.westbowpress.com
1 (866) 928-1240

Unless otherwise noted, scripture quotations taken
from the King James Version of the Bible.

Scripture quotations marked (NIV) are taken from the Holy Bible, New
International Version®, NIV®. Copyright © 1973, 1978, 1984, 2011 by Biblica,
Inc.™ Used by permission of Zondervan. All rights reserved worldwide. www.
zondervan.com The "NIV" and "New International Version" are trademarks
registered in the United States Patent and Trademark Office by Biblica, Inc.™

ISBN: 978-1-9736-6737-7 (sc)
ISBN: 978-1-9736-6738-4 (e)

Library of Congress Control Number: 2019909048

Print information available on the last page.

WestBow Press rev. date: 7/11/2019

Contents

Introduction

◆

If in this book I say anything that sounds like a command, it is just advice. I have no authority to command anyone. This book discusses many topics. If you disagree with something I say, that is okay. I doubt that anyone will agree with everything I say. You may find something else that you like. If you find one thing in this book to be beneficial, then it has been worthwhile. I am an older man. This may be my last chance to say it the way I see it.

Few are likely to read this book. Hopefully it is a blessing for those who do. I believe that I had to go through what I went through to understand what I understand. Sometimes I am a little slow; sometimes I have to learn things the hard way. I write this book from weakness, not from my strength. This book is not about exciting entertainment. I may or may not gain financially, but it is not about me making a lot of money. It is for promoting some understanding that Jesus is real. It is for the least to know they are significant. This is written to say the things I would want to say to my children if I had teenage or older children. It is my duty. Sometimes we should say what needs to be said. Sometimes it seems corny, and we think everyone has heard it, but everyone hasn't. Sometimes no one is observing what we see, so we need to point out a different way. Sometimes we must explain what is misunderstood. Some of what I say comes from the Bible. Some comes from my observations and experience. Some is speculative. Hopefully the speculative things will help you think about something in a better way. Some may be controversial, but sometimes we need to pose questions for contemplation.

Perry Bigbee was a respected businessman in northwest Alabama. He once said something indicating that we can read a story about someone's life. If we see their mistakes and the consequences, we can avoid their mistakes and those consequences. Thank you, Perry Bigbee. I am explaining what I have learned. Maybe it will not take you a lifetime to learn what I have learned. When I speak bluntly, I hope that I do so with some grace. I believe we gain understanding from the Holy Spirit. Thank you, Holy Spirit.

It is important that we say what needs to be said. We may give good instruction to our firstborn child. We should not get lazy and forget to give good instruction to the last child and all those in between.

Embarrassment

Embarrassment can be difficult to overcome. Sometimes it can cause us to do things we should not do. Sometimes we go to great lengths to hide something, not realizing most people already know. Try to keep embarrassment from interfering with doing what is right. When people apologize, we should gracefully accept the apology. Don't be like the reporters who are never satisfied.

Orphans

◆

There have been orphans who became honorable men of great significance. There have also been orphans who became disgusting scoundrels. It is your choice. Becoming an honorable person requires self-discipline. If you are an orphan, if your dad is honorable or a scoundrel, the choice is up to you. You may accept or reject Jesus. I recommend accepting Jesus as the best way. No one can make these choices for you. We will all have failures. We will all go through difficult times. The thing is to learn from our failures and get on with life. When we go through difficult times, we need to consider what God is trying to teach us.

Grace

◆

Grace trumps the law. Grace overcomes the law. It is by grace that we are saved (Ephesians 2:8). It is not just the grace of Jesus. It is also our own grace. We must have the grace to forgive if we are to be forgiven. This does not mean there are no consequences for breaking God's laws. Sometimes we just notice a beautiful woman, and we have sinned. Sometimes we just voice our anger, and we have sinned. Sometimes we are judgmental, and we have sinned. We all fail, except Jesus. Perhaps it is grace if we sometimes get to pay before the judgment. When we try to forgive, in due time we can forgive. Sometimes it takes a while, but with grace and patience, we can forgive. We forgive, and we are forgiven. What goes around comes around. This is the way of Jesus.

Perfection

◆

Many people think that to get to heaven, they must live exactly correctly. This idea is doomed because we all have our failures. Jesus is the only one who accomplished perfection. Certainly we should try for our best, but we always have failures. What can we do? We accept Jesus. We love Jesus. We love one another. We forgive. We share our testimony. We share the good news about Jesus. It is not about being perfect. It is about the love. If we get our life correct 95 percent of the time, that would be a great accomplishment. For me, it would probably be a big improvement. If the operating system in a computer worked correctly 95 percent of the time, it would be worthless. If the operating system was 99.9 percent correct, it would be garbage. If a modem had one error per million bits, it would be unacceptable. If we accept Jesus publicly, we are acceptable!

The Least

❖

Baby chickens may be crowded together for a while. They will start pecking one another. They will get a bloody spot where they have been pecked and then they will all peck the bloody spot. People do something similar. We find that someone is sensitive about something, and we keep pecking at it. I would say we are pushing their buttons. We all have buttons. We should not go around pushing people's buttons. People who are tough in one way will be very delicate in another.

Jesus said, "For he that is least among you all, the same shall be great" (Luke 9:48). If the atom is the smallest particle, then what is the smallest particle of an atom? Let us call the smallest particle of an atom A1. What is the smallest particle of A1? Let us call it A2. What is the smallest particle of A2? Let us call it A3, and so on. Then would dark matter equal A1+A2+A3 …? Scientists say there are four basic forces (gravitational, electromagnetic, strong, and weak). Gravity is the weakest. Certainly gravity affects us more than any of the other forces. Sometimes it is the thing that seems insignificant that turns out to be most significant.

Trinity

◆

Some say Jesus is God. Some say Jesus is the son of God. Some say the Trinity is the Godhead (God the Father, the Son, and the Holy Spirit). Jesus said that He and His Father are one (John 10:30). The three parts of the Trinity are one. The interrelation of the Trinity is beyond our comprehension. That there are three parts does not mean that there is more than one God. They all work in unison. Jesus said, "Why callest thou me good? There is none good but one, that, is God" (Mark 10:18). This seems strange, but remember this was said while Jesus was with us before his Crucifixion. "He saith unto them, But whom say ye that I am? And Simon Peter answered and said, Thou art the Christ, the Son of the living God. And Jesus answered and said unto him, Blessed art thou, Simon Barjona: for flesh and blood hath not revealed it unto thee, but my Father which is in heaven" (Matthew 16:15–17). Thomas said, "My Lord and my God" (John 20:28). This is said after Jesus's transfiguration and resurrection. This means that we should not be suggesting that Jesus is over the God of Abraham, Isaac, and Jacob. If we say that, from our perspective or with respect to us, God and Jesus are one—that is correct.

The Jesus Freak

When I was in ICU, the medication messed up my mind. I thought that something had gone wrong. Something that the doctors would think probably made me a monster maniac. I thought they would never let me go because they thought I could not be allowed back into normal society. The doctors came around a few times with some Asian nurses. I sometimes think Asian ladies are especially pretty. In my mixed-up mind, I thought that if I let on in any way that I thought they were attractive, then the doctors would think for sure that I was a monster maniac. That was a strange situation. Later, I decided that if I was a freak, I would be a Jesus freak. I have always put a high value on the truth. I would not pretend to be someone different from who I was.

I would not dress up in a suit and tie so the ladies would think I was better off financially than I was. In other words, I was not a good salesman. I was not good at getting close to women. Now I am an old man. I still like the truth. Now I know who I am. I am a Jesus freak. When a person gets old, when they are not sure of their own worth and abilities, they can still be a Jesus freak.

Offend

◆

Jesus says, "Woe to that man by whom the offense cometh!" (Matthew 18:7). When we offend, it can cause many problems. We must be as honest as we can; so we try to balance truth and grace. Hopefully we speak truth in love. Some people are so dishonest that they can't accept the truth. Some are determined to be offended. We should try to be graceful and honest, but some will be offended. When we get offended and express that as anger, we can't communicate effectively. In order to change someone's mind, we need to find something we both can agree about. When we do that, we enable the person to understand and agree with us.

King David is considered to have been a great king. He had a great sin, but apparently, he was never prosecuted by the legal system. He continued to be a great king. Perhaps we should remember him when we want to point fingers and criticize the personal lives of politicians.

Don't be too sensitive. Some people will get offended about the least little thing. Everyone does not express everything the same way. Because someone uses a word we do not like does not mean they are bad. Sometimes what we consider degrading does not have the same significance for others. Don't call me sir. I work for a living. My first lesson in the army was not to call a sergeant sir. The sergeant considers it an insult. I realized that I need to be more forgiving to people who are crude and rude. For some people, that is just their personality. Because they are crude and rude does not mean they are wrong. It does not mean they are bad at what they do. It does not necessarily mean that they are bad, mean people. Sometimes that is just the way they express themselves.

Promises

◆

I do not like to make pledges and promises. Sometimes I am weak, and I do not trust myself. Often when politicians make promises, they must either break the promise or do something just as bad. Sometimes it seems like the opposite of what they promise is what happens. Remember the story of the man who asked one son to do something. He said no but then did what was asked of him. Another son was asked to do something. He agreed but then did not do what was asked of him (Matthew 21:28–31). Perhaps it is better to keep promises we do not make than to make promises we do not keep. Some cowboys would say their word is their bond. My mother told the doctor she expected to live to be one hundred. After she turned one hundred, she passed away within the year.

God expects us to keep our promises. God expects us to keep our word. Be careful of what you say. Be careful of what you pray for.

When I was a young man, my dad had lung cancer. He asked me to promise to take care of my mother. I thought that would give him some peace of mind, so I agreed. I did not think much more about it. Years later, I lost a job. I wound up living with my mother until finally I found another job. After that, she lived with me for about twenty-five years before she passed away. During that time when she was living with me, I realized that I should be careful to keep the promise I made to my dad. For me, the idea of looking for a woman to be my wife, getting married, and looking after my mom at the same time seemed impossible. The reality was that she was looking after me as much as I was looking after her. Looking back, I can say it was a blessing for me. We do not know what the details of promises will require. Perhaps we think that we must make promises to function in this world. But we never know what the future will bring.

Murder

◆

Jesus was crucified. Jesus's crucifixion is the ultimate sacrifice for the sins of all people. Jesus, through His resurrection, overcame death. The wages of sin are death (Romans 6:23). Only through acceptance of Jesus can we overcome our sin. The works of our own hands will never be perfect. There will always be a higher level of perfection that people can't accomplish. There will always be something smaller and something bigger than what we can see. It is only by grace that we are saved (Ephesians 2:8). The crucifixion of Jesus seems to mark a time after which people quit sacrificing babies and children through religion. We are saved individually by individually accepting Jesus. Perhaps it is only through societies accepting Jesus that we get away from genocide. We should accept our babies and avoid abortion. Surely it is a terrible thing to kill a baby or child. Surely we are cursed when we do this. Perhaps when people have sex, a spirit wants to be born. Perhaps a soul wants to exist. Choose life.

We have a problem where, occasionally, someone just kills people for no apparent reason. Sometimes a person who is a social outcast just wants attention. Maybe they just want people to know they exist. Sometimes they just want to have their name in the news, even if it is for something bad. Perhaps the news media should quit publishing their names. Socially, they need to find a decent way to be who they are. Jesus is the way, but sometimes society has made being a Christian so rigid that an outcast can't fit in. We need small fellowship groups so everyone can fit in and have a way to discuss difficult situations.

Occasionally, someone kills and says, "God told me to kill that person." They may say that a voice kept telling them to kill someone. Some would say it was not God; it was the devil. Most of us just think that person was crazy. If we think God is asking us to do what we believe to be immoral, we may say no. In the New Testament, Peter sees a vision with a sheet lowering animals. He is told to kill and eat, but he refuses (Acts 11:5–9). If a voice in your head tells you to kill someone, you may say no because it is immoral.

We should not get lost in our legalisms. Doing what is right may not always agree with the laws of people. Our laws and regulations should always connect to the golden rule (Matthew 22:37–40). They should always have that balance. Isn't the United States the kingdom of balance? Wouldn't it be wonderful if we were also the land of grace and truth?

Truth

◆

What benefit is the truth if no one gets it? We need to understand so that we can separate the truth from the lie. In order to be better at separating the truth from the lie, we need to be as honest as we can. What goes around comes around. If we want people to share what they know with us, we need to share what we know with others. There is a time to speak and a time to keep our mouths shut.

We like to have our blessings in abundance. Truth is under restriction. Finding truth requires limitations. If we love the truth, we seek the straight and narrow. Then we can find an abundance of truth. Sometimes when we accept restrictions, we find liberty and freedom.

For every up, there is a down. For every left, there is a right. For every inside, there is an outside. For every lie, there is a truth. The truth and the lie at some point come very close. The difference is so tiny that people have difficulty seeing the difference. Some say the devil is in the details. Some say God is in the details. Perhaps whether something is a lie or the truth is in the details. With time, the lie and the truth usually go in different directions. The truth is correct and accurate. The lie is wrong. We can know them by the fruit they produce. We know them by the end results.

If you understand that what goes around comes around, then you may understand that the more honest we are, the better we will comprehend the truth. Sometimes the military will cover the truth with lies so they can trick the enemy. If anyone uses a lie to get the truth from someone who wants to be honest, they often fail to get the truth. They often just deceive themselves. This is one of the reasons innocent people get convicted for things they did not do. People who use lies to gain advantages in life are more likely to dismiss Christianity. We need to overcome our egos so that we can be humble enough to recognize the truth. When we assume that trickery is being used, that fraud is being pursued to accomplish some twisted purpose, it is startling when we discover there was no fraud. The dishonesty of the human mind makes it difficult to see the truth.

Seeing the truth is like trying to see through a thick fog, and we ourselves are the thick fog.

Theater may be an attempt to accurately depict something that was in the past. Because what was is not here anymore, there is an inherent lie, a misrepresentation, a deception. Certainly actors often misrepresent something; so they have components of a lie, and even though they give some representation of some truth, it is the truth of someone's imagination, not the truth of reality. Usually we get a mixture of truth and lies. We get many shades of gray. Baptism is an indication for the present and the future. The public acceptance of Jesus ties us to the truth, the truth of our future, the truth of Jesus.

Math

If you want to be an electrical or electronics engineer, do not miss the course on j operator (imaginary numbers). We get the idea that these are imaginary numbers because our definition of the square root does not include the square root of negative numbers. We often say plus *or* minus. Perhaps plus *and* minus is also a real situation. In any case, being able to deal with imaginary numbers can result in real solutions for problems.

Understand that when teachers give a definition of a math function, it is necessary, but it is inadequate. There should be an entire course about the math function. Why do we need it? When do we need it? How was this originally discovered? What makes it so powerful? I have never seen this kind of explanation of the math function.

If plane geometry is easy, it does not mean that all of math will be easy. I have heard that those who find geometry easy will have difficulty with algebra and vice versa. If you find one to be easy, you will probably have to work more at the other.

Remember your first works. In the beginning, you learned to count to one hundred one number at a time. Then you counted by twos. Then you counted by fives. I suggest that if you are interested in math, also count by threes, fours, sixes, sevens, eights, and nines. Correct answers may come to mind more easily. When my mind is going where it should not, and I realize what is happening, I count by sevens. The distraction is usually enough to get away from the bad thoughts.

When we read the Bible, sometimes different scriptures seem to be contradictory. It may seem that both scriptures can't be true. Study carefully, and you will find a condition where both things are true. I think of this like solving two equations. The solution leaves only a few correct answers. Or two exclusionary sets leave a small set of possibilities remaining. We want to stay on the straight and narrow. The words that seem contradictory may also be contradictory because of a change in context or timing.

Jesus says something, and we see a meaning in what He said. Then sometimes we find a deeper meaning. We may think it means one thing, and someone else thinks it means something different. We disagree, but often, they are both true. Often things come in threes. We may easily see two, but the third way is difficult to find. The third way is less obvious. Three-dimensional things are more difficult to comprehend than two-dimensional things. Three-dimensional things are defined in terms of ninety degrees. What angle would define the fourth dimension? What angle would define the seventh dimension? No one knows. Fifty-one point four degrees is very close to 360 degrees divided by seven. If we make objects with seven equal sides and seven equal angles using straight lines, these objects will not fit together. They will not fit together in two dimensions, and they will not fit together in three dimensions. There will always be gaps or remainders. The number seven is not special because it fits together. It is special because it does not fit.

Business

My dad told me a story from his youth. He lived near a small town. That town was thriving. Saturday mornings there were crowds of people shopping downtown. Preachers would preach on street corners. Crowds would sometimes listen to the preachers. The town decided this was a problem, and they passed an ordinance to stop the preaching. My grandfather told my dad that he would see a time when the downtown streets would be empty on Saturday mornings. That probably seemed strange to my dad, but that is exactly what happened. Many others can probably find other reasons why this town did not continue to thrive. I suggest that respecting God can be very significant. In our nation, there are many decent people. In our nation, there are many Christians; however, sometimes it seems that our nation is turning away from Jesus.

I tooled leather for many years. The job seemed to me to be the most worthless job a person could do. The job did not provide shelter, transportation, or food for others. It was just decorative. Other people considered it to be art, but to me it was just hard work. Now I understand that art, writing, and mathematics can be ways for someone to say what they should say, and not say what they should not say. I could be bitter about my failures. I could blame others. I could even blame my parents, which would be absurd. Now I understand that getting through my difficulties with my personality gave me a unique perspective, especially when I can get my own ego out of the way. Many people have been through worse or similar difficulties. They also have a unique perspective on life. My difficulties were shaping my destiny. In the past, I sometimes considered my work to be useless, but that brought me to where I am now. Now my duty is to help others know that Jesus is real—the most useful job I can imagine. If I help one person know that Jesus is real, then my life has been worthwhile. Hopefully I help many know that Jesus is real.

Most employers will do something ridiculous that is aggravating. Be patient if you can and keep doing the job. Changing jobs too often can keep us from getting a job when we need it.

If you make a deal for another company to sell your product, and if the deal is such that it is dependent on their profit, they can use unrelated costs to diminish the profit. Perhaps it is better to get paid a fixed amount per item or a percentage of the gross sales.

When I was young, I heard a story about four men. Four men gathered to fix a windmill. They began discussing how they were going to do the job. After a few hours, two of the men had figured it out. They looked around, and the other two men were gone. They found the other two men at the windmill. The other two men had fixed the windmill. There is usually a conflict between the urgency of the job and the need to get it right. Sometimes one way is best; sometimes the other. In my daily work, it seems better to do the easy job first when I can. At the end of the day, I have accomplished something. If I get stuck on the more difficult job, the solution may dawn on me quickly the next morning. If we think we are not qualified to do a job, we may turn down the opportunity to do that job. Later, we may find out that someone much more incompetent is trying to do that job.

We all try to accomplish this or that. In the end, it is just vanity without Jesus. Most of us like to work so that we think we have accomplished something of value. Certainly we should do what we can to help others. We need to limit how much our endeavors separate us from the ones we love. We should limit how much we get separated from God. That is why we need to keep the Sabbath day holy. When our work separates us from our mate, we need a date night.

Rejection

◆

Some reject Jesus. Sometimes people say His timing was all wrong, and they reject Him. They might think He was saying something like, "Wait here. I will be right back." It did sound like He was saying that the generation that He was talking to would see His return. Perhaps they do not realize Jesus had just told the parable of the fig tree. He was probably talking about the generation related to the fig tree

(Matthew 24:32–34).

Some would indicate that there was some time before words were written down. Maybe people just changed what was said to whatever they wanted. Some of the things in the Bible don't fit this idea. Jesus referred to Himself as the son of man. Religious leaders would have wanted him to refer to Himself as the Son of God. Referring to himself as the son of man enabled us to correctly call him the Son of God. He was both. A young man might say, "Don't tell me what to do; I am a man." His dad might correct him, saying, "You are not a man because you say you are a man. You are a man when others say you are a man." Jesus indicated He did not come for peace but to set one against the other (Matthew 10:34–36). Religious leaders would not put that in the Bible; they would probably take it out. Yes, a message that is passed around by word of mouth by people does tend to change. The other possibility is that with the Holy Spirit the meanings of the words become more accurate with time instead of corrupted, as it is with people. We want to say that the Bible is the inerrant Word of God. Certainly it seems to be very accurate. Perhaps, to be correct, we should say the words of Jesus are the inerrant words of God. Each time the Bible is translated, the personality of the translator may influence the subtle nuance of the words. Yes, the dishonesty of humans has some effect. The effect of the inherent dishonesty of humans does not mean that the basic, original, contextual truth does not exist. It does. The distortions of the inevitable misunderstandings of people may influence us today. This is not to suggest that the Bible is not accurate. This is to suggest that the words of Jesus are even more accurate. We each need to read the Bible for ourselves. Our own personality will sometimes allow us to see what others miss. We must also be careful that our own personality does not distort the original truth. We are told not to make assumptions. The problem is that sometimes we assume without knowing that we assumed anything.

Perhaps Jesus intentionally fulfilled the prophesies about the messiah. Even if that is true, that would not mean that He is not the real deal. Could any person do that without being directed by God? When we plug in the electric cord to power an electrical device, we know that the plug with two or three prongs goes into a wall socket. When we connect a computer, the sockets and plugs have more connections. They are often keyed or shaped so that we can't put the wrong plug into the wrong socket. Imagine a connector with hundreds of tiny pins and sockets. The pins and sockets are so tiny and there are so many that we can't possibly line them up with our hands. A guiding mechanism must line up the delicate pins and sockets; otherwise, all the correct connections will never happen. This is like the story of Jesus. No normal person could make the pieces of this intricate story fit without God's guidance. Jesus does not just fit with respect to the golden rule. Jesus fits with respect to what came before His birth. Jesus fits with respect to what came after His crucifixion. Jesus fulfilled the prophesies. Jesus fits like that connector that is too intricate for us to put together of our own ability. Jesus does not fit who people want Him to be. Jesus fits who God wanted Him to be. We just need to accept Him. Give Him a chance in your mind to be who He is. The real Son of the real God. Instead of looking for something that shows that Jesus is a fairy tale, look for what shows that He is real. You will find what you look for. Look for the truth, and you will find Jesus. When we think that we find Jesus is a lie, give it some time, be objective, seek the truth, and you will find that Jesus is true. Jesus reeks of the essence of truth. Jesus did not come to be who we want Him to be. Jesus came to be who He is, the real Son of the real God. Can we overcome our own predisposition to doubt? Yes, we can, but it can be difficult. With God, there is always a way. Jesus is the way.

Some say the world has been here billions of years. Some say the earth has only been here thousands of years. The Bible says a day is as a thousand years, and a thousand years is as a day (2 Peter 3:8). This sounds like a way of expressing multiplication. This sounds like a way to represent long periods of time. Perhaps the seasons of creation are like the layers of an onion. Perhaps in some way we are still in the process of being created. Perhaps we are being ripened or matured into a being that is within the will of Jesus.

Perhaps our souls and spirits are being ripened not just individually but as a society. Perhaps we are going through a process—a process that has seasons. Someday we will be ready to be harvested. Are you ready for the rapture (1 Thessalonians 4:16–17)?

Why does God allow evil to exist? He allows it to exist because we must decide if we accept Jesus. Even if God knows what our choice will be, we must decide. We get a season to decide. Evil will have its season. God will then have eternity. That is simply how it must be for us to exist. What eternity will you choose? Jesus is the better choice. The decisions we make determine who we are. Seek the discernment of the Holy Spirit.

Why is pursuing pleasure a sin? The pleasure does not of itself seem to be a sin. Perhaps with every pleasure there is a responsibility. Perhaps every pleasure has a duty that it requires of us. Perhaps every pleasure has its limitation, beyond which it causes harm and becomes evil. If we eat too much without exercise, we become obese. When we have sex, we should take responsibility for the baby. When we talk too much, we must be honest and humble. When we brag, we should acknowledge that we have our failures.

People are sometimes offended by the level of violence and destruction applied to those occupying the Promised Land. Those people worshipped false gods. Those people integrated sexual activities into their religion. Those people made human sacrifices, burning children to death. Those people earned the wrath of God. Vengeance does belong to God (Romans 12:19).

The golden rule demands equity instead of inequity or hypocrisy. Through Jesus, we know that we reap what we sow (Galatians 6:7). Through Jesus, we know that as we measure, it will be measured back to us (Matthew 7:2). Through Jesus, we know that as we judge, we will be judged (Matthew 7:2). Through Jesus, we know that the merciful will receive mercy (Matthew 5:7). Through Jesus, we know the truth because He gave it freely to everyone. When we publicly accept Jesus, we are accepted by Jesus. This is salvation. After salvation, those who are arrogant will be humbled or humiliated. Those who were humble will be elevated (Matthew 23:12).

With the kings and pharaohs claiming to be god, considering that they claimed to be the sons of god, is it so strange that the real God would send his real Son? The Son of God is described in Isiah 53. In accepting Jesus, we can gain a peace that surpasses all understanding (Philippians 4:7).

Scientists seek a singularity. Perhaps when they find it, it will be what goes around comes around. Perhaps when scientists find the singularity, it will be that the golden rule is not a cute little rule but a cold, hard fact of life. The singularity might be that what we do unto others does come back to us over time. God is not a hypocrite. We are the hypocrites.

The Golden Rule

♦

Some come to Jesus on the Roman road. Some come to Jesus on the Ethiopian road. Some come to Jesus through the golden rule. If someone comes to Jesus in a way we do not understand, that does not mean that they are wrong. Things that are contradictory are not always contradictory in every situation. We tend to think that with two opposing views, one must be true and the other false. That is not always true. Sometimes there is a time, place, or situation where both apparently opposing views are true. Sometimes concepts that appear to be opposing are just complementary. Sometimes our thinking is just incomplete.

The golden rule brings a solid foundation of faith in Jesus. Jesus is "the way, the truth and the life" (John 14:6). The golden rule is "whatsoever ye would that men should do to you, do ye even so to them" (Matthew 7:12). Five similar quotes to the golden rule are listed below:

> With what measure ye mete, it shall be measured to you again. (Matthew 7:2)

> Whatsoever a man soweth, that shall he also reap. (Galatians 6:7)

> With what judgment ye judge, ye shall be judged. (Matthew 7:2)

> Thou shall love the lord thy God with all thy heart, and all thy soul, and with all thy mind. This is the first and great commandment. And the second is like unto it, Thou shall love thy neighbor as thyself. On these two commandments hang all the law and the prophets. (Matthew 22:37–40)

> What goes around comes around. (A common saying, unknown source.)

That is to say that what we do in life will come back to us over time. Perhaps to understand this concept, we could consider that when we drop something, it falls immediately. We know this is caused by gravity. If the fall were delayed unpredictably, we might not understand that gravity exists. Perhaps this unpredictable delay is the way the golden rule works. If we understand a simple idea, then we apply it, and we can understand something more complicated. When a simple idea is applied many times, the end results are complicated. The golden rule is a simple idea. Life is complicated. The golden rule is in our life. The golden rule is in history. The golden rule is in the Bible. If a person looks objectively for the golden rule in their life sometimes, they will see it. With the complexity of life and the delay between cause and effect, we can see only a small part of the effect of the golden rule. Sometimes we can see what seems ironic. Sometimes what returns to its source is so exact that we know it is no accident; so we know it is the golden rule. To understand that the golden rule is real the way gravity is real, observe it in life. When you know that what goes around comes around, then read the book of Matthew and be aware of the words of Jesus, and you will know that Jesus is real.

The golden rule does not just apply to me or you. It applies to everyone and everything. If, in life, we intersect with what is more powerful than we are, we can get crushed. If a nice person stands in the way of a train, that person will get run over the same as anyone else would. What goes around comes around is also related to the inertia of the train. A student of physics might say that for every action there is an equal reaction, opposite in direction. What comes our way is not just a result of what we initiate. What comes our way may include what others have started. What comes our way may include things that just happen. A bridge might collapse, or a storm comes through. Sometimes we are just in the wrong place at the wrong time. Bad things happen to good people. As we measure, it will be measured back to us again. This does not mean that it will return at the time we expect. It will return at the time that is God's will. We live in an intricate world. What goes around comes around is the part we have some control over. What goes around comes around does not mean that everything will come back to us in this lifetime. Yes, for Christians, our works may affect what heaven is for us. Some will be elevated, and some will be humbled (Matthew 23:12). If we want people to be kind to us, we should be kind to them. If we want people to help us, we should help other people. If we want people to leave us alone when we are trying to do something, then we should leave others alone when they are trying to do something. If we want to know the truth, we should be as honest as we can. If we want to be forgiven, we should forgive. If we want to be accepted by other people, we should accept other people. If we want God to hear us, we should listen to Him. The end does not justify the means. The means determines the end. Matthew 7:2 does not indicate that what we measure *might* come back to us. It indicates that what we measure *shall* come back to us. It does not indicate that as we judge, we *might* be judged. It indicates that as we judge, we *shall* be judged.

Matthew 22:37–40 indicates that from the golden rule hangs all the law and the prophets. In other words, prophecy is dependent on the golden rule and the love of God. The future is known because of what happened in the past. What goes around comes around, but it may go many other places before it returns.

"Vengeance is mine; I will repay, sayeth the lord" (Romans 12:19). Just leave it to God, and it will be taken care of. When we resist the desire for revenge and return good for evil, then progress is possible. Jesus died for our sins. When we accept Jesus publicly, He accepts us, and we are forgiven. Jesus is our savior, and through Him, we gain eternal life. When I have doubts, thinking the story of Jesus might just be another fairy tale, I remember the golden rule. I know from observation that what goes around does in fact come around. The story of Jesus has to be true. The golden rule is so ingrained in the teachings of Jesus that He must be real.

I used to have difficulty with the first commandment—to love God. I would think, *I do not choose love; love chooses me.* But love did choose me and you when Jesus was crucified. Commanding love does not seem reasonable. Certainly it would be ridiculous for me to command someone to love me. God can command love because God is God. Command and love don't want to go together. Loving God is necessary. Loving Jesus is what we must get to. Accomplishing an attitude of love for God is the goal. It is like accepting the peace of mind that goes beyond all understanding. We practice and pursue loving God, and then we do love God, we do love Jesus, and we do love the Holy Spirit. What we seek is what we find, but sometimes we find more than we expected. We are saved by the grace of Jesus through the provision He made for us on the cross. We cannot earn and do not deserve this, but we must believe in Him and accept that He died on the cross to save us. Sometimes people say life is not fair. They better hope it is not fair. We can't live righteously enough to deserve salvation. We are saved only by grace. Moses killed a man, Elijah ran away, and Noah got drunk. Not that I have any place to criticize them. I say this to emphasize that the only one who was perfect was Jesus. Life may not be fair, but the balance of the golden rule always exists. Works determine what situation we are saved into. Yes, we can see the golden rule as a warm, fuzzy rule. We can see that it would be nice if everyone followed it. I suggest that what we do unto others does come back to us, whether it is nice and kind or ugly and mean. I am suggesting that it is not just a warm, fuzzy, cute rule. I am suggesting that the golden rule is a cold, hard fact of life. Look for the golden rule objectively, with the eyes of a child, and you will find it. Look for the cause and effect of the golden rule in your own life, and you will find it. Look for the cause and effect of the golden rule in history, and you will find it. Look for the cause and effect of the golden rule in the Bible, and you will find it. Seek and keep seeking until you can see the cause and effect of the golden rule. (What goes around comes around.)

Matthew 7:2 indicates that as we measure, it is measured back to us again. Sometimes it is like our soul is weighed, and the cumulative results are what come back to us. Matthew 7:2 speaks of measuring. Measuring can relate to how much of this or that has accumulated. It can represent a summation of what has happened previously. Our tomorrow will be dependent on how we lived our yesterdays. Today will be our yesterday tomorrow. Today is what we control. We can repent and change our direction if we know when we are going the wrong way. The sooner we repent the better. Sometimes we need to turn around. Sometimes we just need to tweak the direction we are going.

Examples

◆

One afternoon I was driving home. Someone cut in front of me, almost causing a wreck. It made me angry. When I was getting closer to home, a different person drove past me. He was gesturing and was obviously angry. He must have felt that I had done to him what the first person did to me.

Before Rome accepted Christianity, Christians were persecuted. After Rome accepted Christianity, people who were not Christians were persecuted, especially Jews.

I was on a long trip and was aware of people asking for help in Oklahoma City. Knowing where they would be, I put $1,000 in an envelope and gave it to someone on my way back. A few years later, I went on vacation. I stopped at a casino and won $1,000.

I appeared to have contributed to a child being aborted. Regardless whether there was an abortion or not, it caused many difficulties for others. After that, I had terrible times of heartburn off and on for about thirty-eight years. Then I had surgery for cancer of the esophagus. I reaped what I sowed, including emotions of fear and anger. A moment of stupidity can cost us much and can hurt many other people.

When Ronald Reagan was president, he made a point that no one was to be assassinated. He barely survived a gunshot wound.

The Jews came back from Egypt, and they were supposed to completely drive out the people occupying that land. The people who were there sacrificed babies to their gods. They put babies into a fire, destroying them. Sometimes the Jewish people destroyed those people, but sometimes they did not. Because they did not always destroy those people or drive them out, the two societies mingled (Numbers 33:51–53). The Jews then became mingled into the religion of the false gods. The Jews then sometimes put their own babies into the fire. These religions also used sex with the false gods. Sex and death are very powerful forces. When they were confused, people might have put up with the child sacrifices and sex being incorporated into religion. The Jewish communities vacillated back and forth between God and the false gods. When they were faithful to God, it was a blessing. When they pursued the false gods, it was a curse. Remembering that what goes around comes around, perhaps the sacrificing of babies long ago connected in some way to the Holocaust. In the Holocaust, many were burned to death. I do not say this to make any excuse for the Holocaust. Just know that when we do bad things, it can have greater effects than we expect.

Jesus raised Lazarus from the dead, and Jesus was raised from the dead.

We accept Jesus publicly, and Jesus accepts us.

"He that leadeth into captivity shall go into captivity: he that killeth with the sword must be killed with the sword. Here is the patience and the faith of the saints" (Revelation 13:10).

Marriage

◆

We should always respect other people's marriages, whether they do or not. Some men say marriage is just another form of prostitution. There is some truth in that, but the difference between the woman being a slave and her being a partner is huge. The difference is mostly dependent on the man's attitude.

When people get married, they usually make promises. God expects us to keep those promises. I suggest that to get it right, both the man and the woman need to consider their partner to be their equal. Both need to love and respect the other. If a man has more than one wife, will he give any of them the attention they need? Will any of them be able to give him the personal, quality partnership he needs? Most men have difficulty giving the woman enough time, even when they have just one wife. If the man is not well-off financially, he will have to work like crazy just to keep a roof over their heads. If the man is well-off financially, he will have duties that will require his time. However you deal with marriage, remember we are not supposed to leave our first love. Is your first love Jesus? Perhaps our love for Jesus and our love for our first mate are parallel. Perhaps in some way they are tied together. Everyone has every right to be particular about who they marry. Remember the old saying "behind every good man is a good woman." Remember the other saying that "some women can throw more money out the back door with a teaspoon than the man can bring in the front door with a shovel." Be careful of who you choose for a mate. Single blessedness is better than double cussedness. About half of all marriages end in divorce. That also means about half do not end in divorce. Love may sometimes be painful, but that is what life is all about. We should be reluctant to throw away real love just because it is risky. It always is. A good partner will multiply your good works. A good partner will keep you on the straight and narrow.

Someday, you may be a parent. Be careful about the example you set for the children. If you lie, cheat, steal, or harm others, children who see this may think that is what they are supposed to do, especially if you brag about it. My parents made a point of not arguing where we could hear it. Not arguing is a good example for the children.

The Stone

◆

The keystone or cornerstone of an arch is at the top of the arch. It is the stone that holds the arch together. It is the last stone installed. Perhaps the top stone of a pyramid would be considered its cornerstone. When a building is built, the cornerstone is at the bottom. Perhaps it is the keystone of the foundation. When we build our lives on the teachings of Jesus, we are building our house (our life) on rock, not on sand. We then have a foundation that is based on truth. Our life is not based on false placebos or lies used with the power of suggestion. It is based on truth, which is Jesus. "Heaven and earth shall pass away, but my words shall not pass away" (Matthew 24:35). Jesus is the stone that the builders rejected. If we can discover, recognize, or understand that Jesus is truth, then we can accept that Jesus is the cornerstone. The Rosetta stone has writing in three different languages. Because of the Rosetta stone, people today can understand the hieroglyphs of ancient Egypt. It is a stone that was apparently rejected and was later found. We can understand that the Jews were the builders of religion. We can understand that they rejected Jesus. So, Jesus is the stone the builders rejected (Matthew 21:42).

Some may consider demons, angels, and gods. Some may ask, Are they aliens from outer space? Regardless of what they are, whether they are real, or where they come from, they are subordinate to Jesus. Remember the parable of the man who sowed good seed. "The kingdom of heaven is likened to a man which sowed good seed in his field: But while men slept, his enemy came and sowed tares among the wheat, and went his way" (Matthew 13:24–25). Yes, false gods and idols were used with trickery to manipulate and control societies. This does not mean that there is no real God. God is real. Jesus is real. The Holy Spirit is real.

I am not an outgoing person. Sometimes I am slow. Sometimes I am a thinker. Sometimes I continue to consider the things others have rejected. Sometimes I consider what seems ridiculous, and often it turns out that it was indeed ridiculous. Sometimes along the way I find what I did not know I was looking for. In one case, there is truth in what many reject. That one case is that what we initiate in life eventually comes back to us. Some things are just inevitable. God created humans. Then humans tried to create gods. It seems good that God created us and bad that humans made up false gods. That was a part of the nature of people. I worked for electronics engineers. The best electronics engineers are the ones who can get their own ego out of the way of doing the job. When we have a certain view of something, we all have difficulty considering the opposite way. Often, we get things exactly backward. I certainly think the Jewish community, which rejects Jesus, gets it backward—and they think I get it backward. How do we soften their mental opposition to Jesus? The persecution of the Jews by the Catholics did not help. We need to find things we can agree with them about. One thing we can probably agree about is that Isiah 58 gives us good guidelines for living our lives. What Isiah 58 says is not easy, but we will both agree it is right. This process of finding truth always takes time. We need the guidance of the Holy Spirit in order to discern the truth from our own egotistical imagination.

Perhaps some people gain the enlightenment of the morning star. Yes, things do tend to dawn on us in the morning. If that person accepts Jesus and the guidance of the Holy Spirit, then that person will gain better, more accurate enlightenment. Astrology can be disgusting. It can be filled with deceptions, lies, and evil. Is there some truth under all the lies? Yes, but this should only be approached with a very sharp knife. It should only be approached with the discernment of the Holy Spirit. Astrology is a tool, not a religion. Con men can use it with the power of suggestion to trick us. On our own, we can't separate the truth from the lie without seeing the end results. Seek the guidance of the Holy Spirit. When the result is sacrificing babies or abortion, have nothing to do with it, except to encourage repentance. We do go through seasons. God put the stars in the heavens for signs and seasons, and then people tried to make gods out of the planets. Planets are not gods. They are just planets. Astrology may indicate when the things from our past will come back to us. It tells us a season when something may happen. It is probably related to gravity. The gravity signature up to the time of birth combined with heredity may through the DNA determine our personality.

My dad would say love is like gold; it's where you find it. If we seek serendipity, several components contribute to serendipity. Following the golden rule by being kind to others and accepting Jesus is probably the main component of serendipity. Being in the right place at the right time would also be significant. That is when and where. This suggest signs and seasons, which is astrology. The signs and seasons must not be astrology that separates us from Jesus. The planets are not gods; they are just planets. The real God created them. We did not create God. God created us. We do not own God. God owns us. How we do what we do is also important. We need to keep a good attitude. We must be gracious and submit to God's will. We should accept Jesus and the guidance of the Holy Spirit. We need to get our ego out of the way so we can be humble, gracious, and quiet. Then we may sense the discernment of the Holy Spirit. Then what we need to know may dawn on us. When I can't remember something, sometimes the harder I try to remember, the further it is gone from my mind. I must give up and let it go. Later, I sometimes remember. Sometimes we just need to let go of our ego.

If there are real effects from the planets, that suggests some questions. Can we determine the date of birth for our soul mate and then find that person? If we can match the angle between Mercury and Venus, will that equate to love vibes? Maybe it is the angle between Mars and Venus. Maybe it is matching moons. Maybe for some of us, it relates to when and where we were baptized—the time and place where we were born again. Perhaps sometimes we just look for what God brings together.

Is there an astrological relation to autism? Can a child with autism be born again without autism? If we choose to avoid having children with autism, are we eliminating a part of our society that we need? If we only have children with a genius mentality, will they be able to accept Jesus? Perhaps we all need one another. Maybe we need all the shades of gray in between. I tend to get sick in two places. Those two places are in the twelfth and second houses of my natal chart. Does this work the same way for others? Sometimes I remember to be careful when something transits this area. Astrology must be tempered by the truth of the golden rule. Astrology must not be corrupted by the lies of false gods or secrecy. Astrology should not be considered a religion. It is only appropriate as a tool—a tool so that we are prepared to do what is appropriate at the right time and place. We have a date with our destiny. Can we keep that date? Jesus kept His date with His destiny. For us, it is most important to try to live correctly, love Jesus, and love one another. Jesus came to us loving us, teaching us, healing us, and serving us. Sometimes we must surrender, but sometimes we must fight.

Sex

◆

Sex for people has some similarity to the sex that animals have. We are not animals, and we should treat one another with love and gentle kindness. The man should have an attitude of receiving love, not of taking sex. Traditionally, sexual immorality means sex outside of marriage. I speculate that one form of sexual immorality is separating sex from having a baby. I was taught that we do not point a gun at anyone unless we mean it. Maybe we should not have sex unless we mean it, unless we are ready to accept and take responsibility for the baby. The man needs to be able to protect and provide for the woman and the child. Love should also exist. I once heard a woman say she was in it for the money. Years later, I realized that sometimes I need to tell people I am in it for the love. I recommend reading Leviticus chapter 18 from the Bible. Leviticus 18:22 indicates that homosexual activity by men is an abomination. Do not let anyone convince you that the Bible doesn't mention this. We do not have to persecute or mistreat people to say that what they do is wrong. It is not our place to judge them. We all have our failures. Perhaps it is not that Jesus hates homosexuals. Perhaps it is that he loves children. Fantasizing about sex is a lie. I suggest that such behavior makes us vulnerable to tricks and lies.

When I was a young man, I thought that if the woman was okay with sex and I was okay with sex, it would be okay. I was wrong. I was leaving out God. There is something spiritual about sex. If we get it wrong, we can damage our spirit. If we leave out God, we lose the beautiful spiritual aspects of love, and then it just becomes a crude, mechanical, manipulative thing.

When I was a young man, I encountered a woman. We both behaved badly, and she may have become pregnant. The next year, I was falsely accused of attacking someone. For a long time, it did not occur to me that the two events were related. Now I do think the two events were related. Maybe someone wanted revenge. Maybe someone wanted to teach me a lesson. Maybe I just got what I deserved. Perhaps all of those were true. If I had been living more honestly, perhaps others would have been more honest with me. That would have been different. I can't change the past, but I can live in a way that enables the future. There was no way for me to give an honest response. I would want to say yes, sometimes I was woman crazy the way most men are. Yes, I was stupid, but it was and is not my nature to be mean to anyone. Perhaps there were a lot of tricks all around. Tricks begat tricks. Now I want to be extra careful that I do not make any false accusations. I would not want to do to anyone else what was done to me. I forgive the woman, whoever she is. I forgive whoever trumped up the false charge. I forgive anyone who pointed a finger at me and spoke lies. My failure was entirely my own fault, and it would be incorrect for me to blame anyone else. I am not saying others did not have their failures, but if I myself had done what was right, everything would have been much better for everyone.

A bad dream, it just seemed like a bad dream. A man came to my door in the middle of the night. He said the woman was pregnant and might get an abortion. I said that I had no control over what she decided to do. I was wrong. I was wrong regardless of whether she had an abortion or not. What he was saying was so drastic for me that my mind could not accept it. A few years later, when it occurred to me that the false accusation and the woman might be related, I thought, *No, if she was pregnant, someone would have told me.* Sometimes a dream can seem real. Maybe reality can seem like a dream.

Perhaps romantic love is like an electronic oscillator. There are three requirements for an oscillator: (1) There must be a resonating part. The lovers must be on the same wavelength. The lovers are on the same page. They understand each other. They have vibes. They light each other's fire or have a chemistry together. (2) There must also be positive feedback. The lovers make the right connections. They make each other complete. They support each other. (3) There must also be amplification. They must allow God to magnify their complementary spirits, and then they may be successful.

Some people may believe that a person is no good unless he or she gets married. There is probably some truth in that for most of us. The exception would be that there are a few who choose to be celibate. If anyone chooses to be celibate, do they put up treasure in heaven? (See Mathew 19:12.)

There are three who I think would fit choosing to be celibate: Jesus, Paul of the Bible, and J. Edgar Hoover.

The risk of giving our spouse a disease is a good reason to abstain until after marriage. Perhaps we should not have sex with anyone we are not willing to marry. Certainly finding a mate of the opposite sex, marrying that person, and having babies is okay. Perhaps when we have children, boys need to be around men and other boys. Girls need to be around women and other girls. Yes, when they are infants, they both need their mom. Perhaps when they are teenagers, they both need some good guidance from their dad. Why do boys need to be around boys, and girls be around girls? We naturally want what we can't have. If the boy grows up only being around women, when he reaches puberty, he may not see the beauty and desirable characteristics of women, and vice versa. This seems to be one part of what happens at the time of puberty. I do not suggest that it explains everything about puberty.

Each person needs to have some understanding of who they themselves are. If a man does not know his own personality, or if he does not know what he believes, how can he tell a woman who he is? If he wants to be honest, how will he even have a conversation?

Some say that love is not a feeling. Perhaps it is correct to say that love is more than just a feeling. To me, saying love is not a feeling is like saying love is not love. It is like making sex clinical or logical. Surely there must be something immoral about removing our emotions from love and sex. Perhaps our small imperfections are the very things that make us love one another. Perhaps those tiny imperfections are what make us vulnerable and lovable. We do not want to become robots. We do not want to become creatures without souls. For me, if love is not a feeling, it is connected to my feelings, emotions, and affections. Certainly our feelings come and go. Sometimes our affections fade away. We can still understand that we love even when the feelings are weak. Perhaps, to keep the love strong, we must kindle the fire of love with gentle kindness. Perhaps we need to stoke the fire of love with kind words, acceptance, actions, and silly jokes.

Narcotics and Alcohol

When I was a boy, someone told me not to look straight at the sun. The next time I went outside, I tried to look straight at the sun. Why do we do things like this? Why did Adam and Eve eat the forbidden fruit? Why do people get involved with narcotics and alcohol? Perhaps we think we can handle it. We can't. Perhaps we think we are smart enough. We are not. Perhaps we are tempted. Resist temptation. My dad talked a little about narcotics. He indicated that when a person was hooked on narcotics, it was very difficult or impossible for them to quit. I would not say it is impossible, but I would agree it is very difficult. With God, all things are possible. I stayed away from narcotics, including marijuana. I suggest that taking illegal drugs is like Adam and Eve taking the forbidden fruit. It seems to connect to death and murder. We all will die, but most of us do not want to go there before our time. Sometimes people say everyone uses marijuana. That is not true. What they are really saying is that all the people they associate with use marijuana. Perhaps they need to also associate with some different people. When I was in Vietnam and the subject of getting high occurred, one of the soldiers would say, "I just get high on life."

Alcohol was a problem I did have some experience with. It is not just a problem of drinking and driving. At some point, if a person drinks too much, they will go over a mental threshold. After going over that threshold, the person will remember little or nothing.

If they lie down and pass out, when they wake up, they do not know what they have done. They usually do not realize that they did things they would not consciously do. They usually do not know that a piece of time when they were active is completely gone from their memory. If someone tells them that they did something unusual, they do not believe it. They do not know that they do not know what they have done. This is dangerous. For a man, it is dangerous for his wife. Drinking is often connected to a man beating his wife. If the woman drinks too much, it can be unsafe for the man. Usually the woman is a binding, stabilizing force for the family. How can she do that if she drinks too much?

When I was in the service, one day another soldier stopped me to talk for a few minutes. He asked me if I remembered a previous event. He said that one night when I was drinking, I picked up another soldier and threw him onto a top bunk. I thought he was pulling my leg. Thinking that someone is joking with you is a very common response to this situation. Now I look back, and I know better how this works. Did I pick up someone and throw him onto a top bunk? I probably did. When we are in a social situation where others want to drink alcoholic drinks, we can say, "I don't handle alcohol that well." Some may do better than others, but the truth is none of us handle alcohol that well. Most people will respect this statement. If people want to insist that you drink anyway, you are probably with the wrong people. In social situations, drinking can spin out of control very easily. Drinking alcohol when we are emotionally upset just makes a bad situation worse. A tiny amount of alcohol may sometimes be good for us, but large amounts seldom are. The only exception might be if a person has a super bug. If the doctors cannot treat the super bug, then drinking alcohol might make sense. Trying to outdrink someone or gulping down alcohol the way college students sometimes do is dangerous. Fun can be had in many ways. We do not have to go to a bar or a party to have fun. We can get in trouble at a Baptist church on Main Street at high noon. But the odds of getting in bad trouble go way up when we go to a back-alley bar at midnight.

The One Thing

❖

One thing will not be forgiven (Matthew 12:32). The one thing that is not forgiven is to disrespect the Holy Spirit. I confess that I did this. Never, never, never do this. Not long afterward, I reconsidered. I said a prayer: "Lord, if I cannot be forgiven, let me pay for it in this lifetime, so I will not burn in hell." I believe I did pay for it. When we are at the gates of hell, we need to turn around and go the other way. Remember, with God, there is always a way. It may not be an easy way, but there is a way.

When I was in Vietnam, I was only involved in one fight. One night when I was the CQ, someone came into the office and told me that I needed to go to my barracks area. There was a fight. Two men, both outranking me, had been fighting. I had to stop the fight. I got close to them and told them to stop. One of them asked, "Who are you?" I said that I was the CQ. To my surprise, they both stopped and listened to me. I asked where each of them bunked. They were at opposite ends of the company area in different barracks. I was concerned that after I was gone, they might return and start fighting again. I told them to go to their own place and not come back that night. I did not intend for them not to go to the office and the dispensary for medical treatment, but one of them took it that way. I did not enter the event into the log. If I had, they may have both been busted. Later, the company first sergeant made a point that we were to enter all events in the log when we were the CQ. He made that point talking to the entire company while we were in formation. If he had talked to me individually, I might have told him what happened. If I had told him what happened, he might have been expected to bust me and the ones who were fighting. The first sergeant was smart enough not to ask directly but to tell me directly, where it was inconvenient for me to respond. If you are ever in a management position, you could have a similar problem. You must correct someone, but if they admit to doing something, you might be expected to fire them or do something you don't want to do. Later, one understood and appreciated not getting busted. Another soldier and I got an in-country R&R. We went to a different base for a few days. At this base, there was what was referred to as the meat market. It was not a butcher shop. It was where a woman could be found for sex. I was careful, as I had been told to use a condom and wash afterward with soap and water. The problem is we can't put a condom over our soul. We can't put a condom over our spirit. Perhaps that damaged my spirit. Perhaps that was what brought me to a situation where I did the one thing that is not forgiven. Our body is not the only thing we must be careful about. What about the spirit of the child that wants to be born?

Television Sermons

❖

On Sunday mornings I like to watch sermons on television all morning. A person can find preachers they identify with and watch them. This has gradually given me a better understanding of Christianity. I suggest that would be good for teenagers. Of course, it can be good for any of us. Perhaps we could record some of these sermons when they conflict with other activities, like going to church. Preachers and priests do not always get it right. Do not worship them; they are our fellow servants. Respect them and appreciate what they do for us. Yes, if you become a Christian, you receive the gift of salvation, which none of us deserve. It does not mean that your life will be all roses and lollipops. It does not mean that you are getting a free ride that will cost you nothing. Jesus suffered for us, and certainly we will suffer for Him. Christianity is wonderful. It has a foundation in truth. If you like the truth, it is for you. Each person must decide for themselves what they believe. Some churches in the past tried to force people to be Christians. This seems inherently counter to what Christianity is. Each person must accept Jesus of their own free will.

Remember, we need to forgive and be forgiven. Many television preachers can't resist trying to sell something. Forgive them when they do that. Just think of it as intermission. The sermon is not about the messenger; it is about the message. The only exception is when Jesus is the messenger. Most Christian preachers will admit that they sometimes have failures, and of course, we all have failures. Because someone gets something wrong does not mean they get everything wrong. Who are we to judge them? TV preachers have advertisements saying, "For a contribution of so much, we will send you this book, this video, or this thingamabob." Many see this and conclude they are just in it for the money. Because of the money, many may dismiss Christianity. Usually we have already seen their best when we saw the sermon. I suggest that we should sell our books at the bookstore, not from the pulpit. Many of us are easily offended by salesmen. I do not know what the correct answer is for funding television ministries. I just know that with God there is always a way. Perhaps it was inevitable that people would try to create gods. We were created by God. What goes around comes around. We do not exist to create gods. We are here to accept God. Perhaps it is a part of the subconscious nature of people to want to control or create gods. Perhaps how we connect and relate to God and gods influences how God connects and relates to us. Who are we to tell God what to do? Can we be God's people? Can we accept Jesus? We understand God from the perspective of our own personality. Each of us must understand and relate to God in our own way. Each of us needs to read the Bible repeatedly for ourselves. Then our soul and spirit are reformed in better understanding and acceptance of God.

Surrender

We want this; we want that; we want the other. Why do we want things? Perhaps it is because we can't have them. Sometimes we must give something up before we can have it (Matthew 10:39). Adam and Eve took the forbidden fruit. Perhaps they were not ready. Perhaps they did not have the wisdom and maturity to deal with the forbidden fruit. Perhaps the forbidden fruit always brings jealousy, greed, disease, and death. Sometimes we must wait on the Lord because it is not our time. It is not our season. Even though we know that what goes around comes around, we must put curbs on our own selfish desires. We must give those up before we can have them. Otherwise, we will not function properly in society. We will not be able to fit into a community. The Bible says that we must overcome. I think that is talking about overcoming our own selfish desires so that they are not evil. We need to be content. When we can't find someone to be our wife or husband, we need to be thankful for our solitude.

Why does a child understand what a grown person can't accept? A grown person sees something and rejects it. The child will accept because their ego has not developed enough to dismiss things the way we do.

The book of Revelation in the Bible can be very difficult to understand. A warning is in that book. Because of the warning, I am reluctant to discuss the book of Revelation. I certainly do not want to speculate about its meaning (Revelation 22:18–19). I am not suggesting that I understand Revelation. I am just saying be careful even discussing it.

There was a funeral for a child. There was a line of people going by the parents. I knew that I should say something comforting. I could think of absolutely nothing to say. How can we give support to someone who has had the devastating loss of a child? Sometimes God requires of us losing that which means the most to us. Abraham was asked to sacrifice his son. Sometimes we lose a child, and it seems pointless. God's ways are higher than our ways. God's thoughts are higher than our thoughts (Isaiah 55:8–9). Life is a gift. It belongs to God. When He takes it back, be glad for the time it was available. Even if what we have lost is a child.

Secrets

◆

Secrets and lies are not the same thing. Perhaps it would be preferable for people who are required to keep secrets to just say, "I can't talk about that." Understand that if you take a job that involves secrets, some people may assume that you are agreeable to lying. If you like to be as honest as you can, then you may want to discuss this before taking the job. Understand that if your job involves secrets, then secrets will be kept from you and about you. We all must keep some secrets. I suggest that even God has secrets. For us, secrets tend to be temporary; they are kept for a season. My mother would say, "If more than one person knows something, it is not a secret." Pictures of George Washington show him with his mouth tightly shut. There is a time to speak.

There is also a time to keep our mouths tightly shut. We may see that the government has done this or that secretly. We may understand that there will be unintended consequences. If we have agreed to keep our mouths shut, we should keep our mouths shut. Intended consequences will also occur. Sometimes we should keep our mouths shut, even though we did not agree to keep our mouths shut. When someone gives us information in confidence, we generally should not repeat that information. We should not gossip. Sometimes we think we know something, but we have it all wrong. This may appear to be a tell-all book, but some things are not mine to tell. When I was a boy, I said something crude at the supper table. My older brother Phillip told me to shut up. I did. I wasn't going to say a word. He realized what I was doing and did something to make me laugh. No way was I going to let him win that battle. I decided to say no more than was necessary. Now I realize that when he told me to shut up, it was some of the best advice I ever received. Heaven only knows how much trouble that kept me out of.

Secrets may, for a time, give some people power. Some societies used tricks with false gods to control people. When people thought the king was a god, then the king gained power over the people. Eventually, people realized that the king was just another man. Then the power of the kings began to diminish.

My dad took me to a prison somewhere in Oklahoma. We went into the prison, and I waited while he went farther inside. He talked to one of the prisoners. Then he came back, and we left the prison. The house where we lived had a one-car garage, which my dad used for a saddle shop. The prisoner he had talked to came and worked for my dad. It gave him a transitional path from prison back into society. One day, my dad told me not to tell my mother that the man had been in prison for murder. I did not tell my mom that the man had been in prison for murder. My dad was a good man.

Suicide

◆

When I was in Vietnam, one night I was on guard duty. It was raining. At that moment, I was aware that success in life for me was unlikely. I considered that my M-16 was right there, and I could end it all if I wanted to. Instead, I stepped out of the guard shack and stood in the cold rain. I was wet and cold. I stepped back into the guard shack. After my guard shift, I was cold and uncomfortable. I went inside, lay down on a canvas army cot, covered up, got warm, and went to sleep.

The other time suicide came to mind was years later, before I had a difficult surgery. We never know what the future will bring, success or failure or a purpose in life that we never imagined. I have heard about people who can't forgive themselves. I suggest it is not about forgiving ourselves. We live with it. We get through it. We accept the forgiveness of Jesus. I do not know what the future brings. None of us know. Maybe I will live thirty minutes. Maybe I will live another thirty years or more. I hope to finish this book. The main thing is that I know that Jesus is real. That brings me much peace of mind. Where we think we are going in life may be very different from what Jesus intends. I used to be an electronics technician in Texas. I never imagined that I would be tooling leather in Alabama for twenty years. I did.

Sometimes we must be able to reject our rejections in order to be able to accept acceptance. In this life, there will always be some people who reject us and some people who accept us. This is true whether we are handsome, healthy, and outgoing or if we are ugly, broken, and withdrawn. How many people reject or accept us will vary, but both situations will exist. If one person understands that Jesus is real because of you, then your life is worthwhile. Sometimes finding a desirable situation in life is difficult, but don't give up. Be a survivor.

Exploitation

❖

Sometimes people are enslaved for sex or labor against their will. Have no part in that kind of exploitation of people. Certainly it is a terrible curse on anyone who takes part in this kind of exploitation. What benefit is there if a person gains the whole world but loses their soul (Matthew 16:26)? People who are involved in this kind of exploitation should let those people go free. Apparently, enslaving people for sex or work even exists in the United States. For it to exist as it apparently does suggests that some component of organized crime exists.

Employers should not take advantage of employees. Employees should not take advantage of employers. It works both ways. Employers usually have the power.

We should not ask others to lie, cheat, steal, or harm other people.

I realized that Isiah 58 is special to some of the Jews. I decided to read Isiah 58 occasionally, hoping that someday some of the Jews would read Isiah 53. Isiah 58 has fourteen verses, not very long. I find it rather difficult. It starts out telling us to lift up our voice like a trumpet, telling our people their transgression. I am not a very outgoing person, so for me it will probably require some work. Isiah 58 also speaks about oppression and mistreating workers. It says we should break every yoke. Employers often take advantage of workers, so this is understandable. Isiah 58 also says that we must not point fingers. Lifting up our voice like a trumpet and not pointing fingers may seem contradictory. A trumpet is loud. It is public, and everyone hears it. A trumpet is used at the right time and place. We are not to point fingers. In other words, don't single out individual people. We should speak against the sin, not against specific people.

Abortion

◆

The Jews would sometimes turn away from God and worship idols. They would throw babies into a fire and let them burn to death, sacrificing to those idols (2 Kings 17:17). These practices brought curses, not blessings. King Herod, according to the Bible, killed children. He was trying to destroy Jesus. King Herod died only a few years later. In our time, the government made abortion legal. Children are destroyed even before being born. They are sacrificed for convenience (see Luke 23:28–29). I once overheard a Mormon lady say, "Sex is for having babies." This may seem incomplete, but certainly there is some truth in that statement. Choose life. Sex does not just relate to having babies. Sex also relates to being accepted. We all want and need to be accepted. We need to accept Jesus. Accepting Jesus means that we will be accepted by Jesus, but it also means some people will reject us because we are Christians. We need to accept other people. We need to accept people of the opposite sex. We need to accept babies and children. We need to be kind and forgiving. We should not pursue stupidity; in other words, we should not keep doing what encourages bad behavior. We should not encourage bad behavior for ourselves or others.

Stupidity

---◆---

The Bible often says, "Fear not." The Bible, as far as I know, never says to be stupid. When Jesus was being crucified, He said, "Father forgive them; for they know not what they do" (Luke 23:34). When we sin, it is often because of bad reasoning and misunderstanding. I suggest stupidity is the cause of many sins. We are all stupid compared to Jesus. Are we smart enough to know we are stupid? We are probably smarter when we know we are stupid. If a man becomes so smart that he can move great stones easily, he would still be stupid compared to Jesus.

"For now we see through a glass, darkly" (1 Corinthians 13:12). Each of us sees just a small piece of the life that is going on around us. We tend to think that others know all the things we know, but they do not, and we do not know all of what they know. We all have different abilities. We like to think that we have everything right, but we all make mistakes. Sometimes it takes some self-control to consider what others believe. We can learn something from anyone, even our worst enemies.

Blood

❖

Jesus told His disciples to eat whatever was set before them (Luke 10:8). What we eat should not interfere with sharing the good news about Jesus. Yes, a vegetarian diet makes sense. If we avoid eating blood, as suggested in the Old Testament, that might suggest not eating anything that has blood (Genesis 9:4). This would separate us from killing. In the time of Isaiah 11, the lion will eat hay. We will probably not eat animals. What we really live by is what comes out of our mouth, our words (Matthew 15:11). Perhaps it would be better if we could have self-discipline about both what we eat and what we say. I suggest that our blood is the ground circuit for the nervous system. This would agree with the idea that the soul is in the blood.

Vengeance

❖

Vengeance belongs to God (Romans 12:19). When we want revenge, we do not want an eye for an eye. We want a hundred eyes, a thousand teeth, and buckets of blood. Even if we did want an eye for an eye, no human could measure such a thing, not even a judge. The Bible says that not one jot or tittle will pass from the law (Matthew 5:18). We are not capable of measuring jots and tittles. We are just able to forgive. Sometimes forgiving seems impossible. If we resist our desire to vent or pursue revenge, then with time we may accomplish a forgiving attitude. Returning good for evil is always the right thing to do.

History

---◆---

If you have difficulty with grammar, as I do, you might not want to pursue history classes at the university. From my perspective, university history teachers are like English teachers. The exams require writing as fast as possible to get everything down on paper. The exams leave little or no time to make grammar corrections and may result in bad grades.

Conclusion

What goes around comes around. That is not the only thing that comes our way in our life. We will also encounter what others initiate. We will also encounter what just happens (Luke 13:4). Bad things happen to good people. What we ourselves initiate is what we have control over. How we respond to others is what we have control over. The golden rule is one part of life. The effects of what others initiate and what just happens because of a physical situation can also affect our lives. We should also consider Ezekiel 33:12 (NIV), "Therefore, son of man, say to your people,' if someone who is righteous disobeys, that former righteousness will count for nothing. And if someone who is wicked repents, that person's former wickedness will not bring condemnation.

The righteous person who sins will not be allowed to live even though they were formerly righteous." This was before Jesus. Through Jesus, we are under grace; however, a person who accepted Jesus can reject Jesus, and a person who has rejected Jesus can accept Jesus. Don't let go of the love of Jesus!

Did I get everything in this book correct? Probably not. I am just another stupid, weak man. If I did get a few things correct, it is because of the guidance of the Holy Spirit. Now I know Jesus is real, and sometimes I have peace of mind that is incredible. There will be good times, and there will be bad times. Your decisions are for you to make. Do not blame me. Do not blame your parents. Do not blame the preacher. Take responsibility for the decisions you make.

My dad was a good man. One evening, he noticed a car on the road across from our house. It was a four-lane road, and we lived on the service road. He went over and found that a young lady was in the car, and it was broken down. That was before cell phones. She did not know what to do and was afraid. My dad got her to give him her dads' phone number. He told her he would go call her dad. She said, "But you do not know my dad." My dad replied, "Oh yes, I know him." My dad had never met her dad, but he knew him in the sense that her dad would want to keep her safe. After calling her dad, my dad parked behind her and waited until her dad came and took her home safely. It is easy for me to honor my mom and dad. We should find a way to honor our mom and dad. If we don't honor them, how will we honor our heavenly Father? Do we think that God has no duties that are beyond our ability to comprehend?

When I was young, I considered that what goes around comes around. I liked to go out for breakfast. Being alone in a restaurant did not bother me. One day, I went to a restaurant and was sitting in a booth waiting for breakfast. Two men were in a booth nearby. They were talking. One said, "Every time I give more to the church, my business does better." I had difficulty keeping from laughing out loud. I felt like rolling in the aisle with laughter. The context was so different from the way I had been thinking about *what goes around comes around* that it seemed ridiculous. I had not been thinking of it in relation to money. Does the philanthropist give away money because they are wealthy? Is the philanthropist wealthy because they give away money? Perhaps the answer to both questions is yes. In any case, we need to be good stewards of the money. In Oklahoma, I gave $1,000, and eventually it came back to me. How do we leverage the situation for accomplishing real good benefits? Not just benefits for our own greedy desires but blessings that give significant help to others. Perhaps we must testify for Jesus.

Our testimony spreading the good news of Jesus might multiply the blessings. We should not allow the pursuit of money to interfere with doing what is right. Remember, we have more to give than money. Jesus gave His life for us. We need to be kind. We need to be graceful. We need to be honest. Sometimes Jesus shows us things we did not expect. Each time we read through the Bible, we notice things we did not see before. We come to Jesus and understand Him best when our attitude is like that of a child. If we want to use a horse, someone must break the horse. Sometimes we must be broken before Jesus can use us. When I was in intensive care at the hospital, I decided that if Jesus was done with me here, it was okay. If he had something else for me to do, it was okay. Now I'm writing this book.

If you do not believe, or have doubts, that Jesus is real, I suggest that you privately and secretly ask the Holy Spirit to help you understand if Jesus is real. Keep it secret for some time. We do not know what the gestation time will be. Remember, if you want God to hear you, you should listen to Him. You have nothing to lose and everything to gain. When we understand that what goes around comes around, that it is the same as the golden rule, that it is natural, real, and mysterious the way gravity is natural, real, and mysterious, then we may appreciate Jesus. Beware of people and organizations that want to control or manipulate you. Beware of people and organization that want to get your money. Beware of people and organizations that say, "Trust me." Only Jesus is qualified to say that. This is not to say these are necessarily all bad; just be careful. Beware of preachers who seldom mention Jesus. How can they preach Christianity if they are reluctant to mention Jesus? Remember, we are not just supposed to pray for our friends and relatives. We are supposed to pray for our enemies (Matthew 5:44). We should not just pray for our president when we like him or her. We don't just pray for the president when the president agrees with us. We don't just pray for our country. We also pray for Russia and Israel.

We inevitably reach a point where we can't comprehend a principle within our own ability to understand. At this level, we must accept the truth. We must have faith. We accept God the Father, the Son, Jesus, and the Holy Spirit. They make us three-dimensionally whole—spirit, body, and soul. Because of them, we exist. We must accept God. We must accept Jesus. We must accept the Holy Spirit. We must accept being forgiven. We must accept our duties. We must accept grace. We must accept love. We can only have the benefits of these by accepting them.

For Jews, I recommend Isaiah 53 for a description of Jesus.

For Muslims, I say Jesus loves you. Where is the love in your religion? Where is the forgiving? God created us. That makes him our Father.

Sometimes I like to think that when God looks down and sees how ridiculous we are, He rolls with laughter. I hope so.

Now it is time for me to park my pen, so I leave you with one last consideration. Yes, what goes around comes around; it is real. But we are to have agape love. We love our enemies. We love even when we are rejected. We love without any expectation of a return. We do not know what the future brings, but we love anyway.

All Bible quotes are from Bible Gateway (biblegateway.
com) KJV.

Ezekiel 33:12 is from Bible Gateway (biblegateway.
com) NIV.

Printed in the United States
By Bookmasters